OBTAINING THE ANOINTING

It is for you!

OBTAINING

THE

ANOINTING

It is for you!

I0086178

KEITH
INGRAM

LAURUS BOOKS

OBTAINING THE ANOINTING

It is for you!

BY KEITH INGRAM

Library of Congress Control Number: TXu 1-173-702

Paperback: ISBN: 978-1-943523-36-8
Mobi (Kindle): ISBN: 978-1-943523-37-5
ePub (Nook, iBooks): ISBN: 978-1-943523-38-2

Published by LAURUS BOOKS

LAURUS BOOKS
A DIVISION OF THE LAURUS COMPANY, INC.
www.TheLaurusCompany.com

This book may be purchased in paperback from TheLaurusCompany.com, Amazon.com, and other retailers around the world. Also available in formats for electronic readers from their respective stores.

Dedicated to those

possessing hungry hearts

for God.

May you be filled.

Foreword

I did not graduate from Yale, nor did I receive a degree in business. I am not alone, however, because neither did the Apostle Peter. Peter was a fisherman, a simple working man, yet God used him to write books in the Bible.

The Scriptures say in Acts 4:13: "Now when they saw the boldness of Peter and John, and perceived that they were unlearned and ignorant men, they marvelled; and they took knowledge of them, that they had been with Jesus."

There is nothing wrong with a great education. We see it daily in the lives of men and women of God. The prophet Samuel went to Eli's Bible college, and Paul went to Gamaliel's. If God has been leading you that way, it is a great thing.

Proverbs 1:7 warns that "fools despise wisdom and instruction." And remember that Romans 12:3 says, "For I say … to every man that is among you, not to think of himself more highly than he ought to think …" because if a man thinks he can stand without Christ, let him "take heed lest he fall" (1 Corinthians 10:12).

Your Brother in Christ,
Keith Ingram

Preface

Praise the Lord! I hope that this book, ***Obtaining The Anointing, It is for you!*** is a blessing to you and your family. I pray that it will encourage you to want to do more for God and that it causes you to want to grow in the anointing. I believe that you have not obtained this book by chance and that it has been placed in your hands to propel you toward a closer walk with God.

This book was written to encourage God's people to want a closer walk and a greater walk with Him. I stand on the belief that Jesus Christ was not only the Son of God, but He *was* God. According to 1 Timothy 3:16: "And without controversy great is the mystery of godliness: God was manifest in the flesh, justified in the Spirit, seen of angels, preached unto the Gentiles, believed on in the world, received up into glory."

Chapter One

I will share what I have experienced besides being saved and filled with the Holy Ghost!

One day, I walked by the radio and said, "That's my favorite song playing." The anointing of God began to fall as if it were being poured out of a bucket. It ran down my head and felt like water, then drips of fire. I could not speak even though I tried. Then I felt it run down my face and onto my chest.

Sometime later, I recall a brother from the church picking me up at my home one evening, and we went to pray for a member of his family. He told me that his aunt was in desperate need of prayer. Upon arriving at their home, a few people were there, and when I walked in, I saw maybe four sitting in one room and six in another. They pointed out his aunt and asked me to please pray for her.

The anointing came upon me as I walked to where she stood, and she was slain in the spirit under the anointed power of God. Those in the room said they could feel God there, and those in the other room said they could feel God in a strong way. The only way I can describe how I felt was like a lampshade had been placed over my head.

Another night, I was in a church service in Tennessee, and people were dancing and praising God. I thought, *If that is real, God, I want it, too.* Right then, the Spirit led me to the front of the church where others were praising God. I looked at the pastor. His eyes were very dark brown, but I saw them turn to a very bright green. The Spirit and power of God came out from his eyes and entered into my eyes and filled my body. I then began to dance in the spirit and could not stop. Our God is "The Lord of the Dance"!

Many years later, I was in North Carolina in a tent revival. The man of God, Rev. James Ward, asked if anyone else needed prayer. I did not go up to the altar, even though I wanted to. His hand was raised, and I saw a ball of fire in his hand. That ball of fire hit me in the head! I was carried out in the Spirit into a quiet place.

I have been in church services and had God take me into a spiritual realm. Many times, I could see the people around me but could hear only the wind. I recall one time in particular. I went to the church to pray and didn't think anyone was around. As I was praying, I turned, and there stood a man. I had not heard anyone come in. I wondered what he wanted. Maybe directions to some place in town? Or was he wanting to see the pastor? He stood there briefly and then vanished. I was so frightened that I fell down and began to worship God. Yet, I wondered why he never spoke!

I can only remind myself of Isaiah 55:8-9: "For my thoughts are not your thoughts, neither are your ways my ways, saith the Lord. For as the heavens are higher than the earth, so are my ways higher than your ways, and my thoughts than your thoughts."

I have experienced other things that I cannot mention because they are personal and between God and me.

Who can be saved? We read in Revelation 22:17, "And the Spirit and the bride say, Come. And let him that heareth say, Come. And let him that is athirst come. And whosoever will, let him take the water of life freely." Do you want the anointing?

The cost for the anointing is living right and serving God with a pure heart. God anoints only the dead in Christ. You must die to the flesh. John 3:30 states: "He must increase, but I must decrease." Nevertheless, if there is not a call of God on your life, you can fast every day, as the Spirit leads.

You have to find the place where God wants you in the body, His body. We are all the body of Christ. You need to find your place in the anointing and abide in it. Be faithful to the call of God that He has placed on your life.

You may never prophesy or run the aisles, and that's all right, but you need to answer when God calls. God may use you in the spiritual gifts spoken of in 1 Corinthians 12, such as the word of wisdom, the word of knowledge, faith, gifts of healing, miracles, prophesies, discerning of spirits, tongues, or the interpretation of tongues. "But one and the same Spirit works all these things, distributing to each one individually as He wills." (1 Cor. 12:11 NKJV). One commentary states that "although these gifts are unequal, yet they are most wisely divided, because the will of the Spirit of God is the rule of this distribution."

Once you are born again, a call is placed upon your life.

Matthew 7:7-8 states: "Ask, and it shall be given you; seek, and ye shall find; knock, and it shall be opened unto you: for every one that asketh receiveth; and he that seeketh findeth; and to him that knocketh it shall be opened." They shall be filled. God said in Jeremiah 29:13 (NKJV): "And you will seek Me and find Me, when you search for Me with all your heart."

How hungry are you? God's words bear out that we should **pray** and **study** every day, and that we should **fast** as the Spirit leads.

The Bible says that Phillip went to Samaria and preached Jesus, and the Spirit led him to an Ethiopian eunuch. Let us be led of the Holy Spirit.

Jesus said He is the Spirit of truth and that He will lead

and guide you unto all truth!

Remember, it's the anointing that destroys the yoke, not *breaks* it but *destroys* the yoke, whatever is binding you. The anointing is like the Word of God: the letter (the law) kills, but the Spirit quickens. It *brings to life*. The body without the spirit is dead. With the Spirit, the anointing, it is alive. For we live not without Him living within us.

Now, I like good singing, but songs alone won't do it. It will not cause you to completely forget your problems. Though it may last for a while, they will come right back to mind. Only through the anointing will they be destroyed forever!

You can take a little child or someone who can't even sing, and they might sing "Jesus loves me this I know, for the Bible tells me so," and this may cause someone to come to the altar. A soul is saved or filled with the Holy Ghost because of the anointing upon that one life. Therefore, they are no longer singing to man but unto God!

Who can obtain the anointing? All can, and it is for you! So quit seeking the anointing, and start seeking the Anointer.

The Bible says Moses wished not, knew not, that he had the anointing of God. He did not seek the anointing but the Anointer. You will never walk in the anointing by some preacher or other great men of God pouring oil upon your tongue or head. That alone won't do it! You have to have a relationship with God for yourself first.

I began writing this book as I was doing other things, and the Spirit moved upon me. God showed it to me for me, but Jesus said freely you have received, freely you shall give. For these things were not done in a corner. I have learned that we go through things sometimes in order to help others. God is molding you into the image of His Son, Jesus Christ, from the moment you get saved, and if Christ walked in the anointing, God wants us to do likewise.

Chapter Two

I remember one time we were in a tent revival in Greenville, Tennessee, ministering with the man of God, Rev. Dewey Ward. A man came up for prayer and was walking with two hand canes. He was an elderly man, and his legs looked very bad. After receiving prayer, he hobbled off. Then Pastor Ward said, "Get his canes." I thought he was going to fall as they took one away. He did almost fall. Then Rev. Ward said, "Get the other one, too." The man began to sag, then stood up straight, and started running and praising God. He was instantly healed! Hallelujah!

The anointing of God is very precious and not to be taken lightly. I call to your remembrance Exodus 35-40 of the construction of the tabernacle of God. God had given Moses precise instructions on how it was to be built, and Moses carried out those instructions precisely. I encourage you to read these chapters. God was very particular about how the tabernacle should be made.

God does not dwell in a tent! He dwells in man! First Corinthians 6:19 says: "What? know ye not that your body is the temple of the Holy Ghost which is in you, which ye have of God, and ye are not your own?"

God will not dwell where there is sin. Even the priests, before they could enter into the holy place, had to wash their hands and feet. If they entered without washing, they would fall dead. We can learn from this. Today, God wants men and women with clean hands and feet. He wants them clean in their lives, what they do and where they go.

One cannot confess Jesus Christ as their Savior and dabble in sin. Hebrews 12:1 says: "… let us lay aside every weight, and the sin which doth so easily beset us …" If you want to walk in the anointing, it is critical that you are holy as He is holy.

First Peter 1:13-16 tells us: "Therefore gird up the loins of your mind, be sober, and rest your hope fully upon the grace that is to be brought to you at the revelation of Jesus Christ; as obedient children, not conforming yourselves to the former lusts, as in your ignorance; but as He who called you is holy, you also be holy in all your conduct, because it is written, 'Be holy, for I am holy'."

We can learn from the tabernacle of Moses that we read about in Exodus. In 1 Peter 2:9-10, we read: "But ye are a

18

chosen generation, a royal priesthood, an holy nation, a peculiar people; that ye should shew forth the praises of him who hath called you out of darkness into his marvellous light; which in time past were not a people, but are now the people of God: which had not obtained mercy, but now have obtained mercy." And in verse 11, we hear the heart cry of God: "Dearly beloved, I beseech you as strangers and pilgrims, abstain from fleshly lusts, which war against the soul ..."

"For the earnest expectation of the creation eagerly waits for the revealing of the sons of God" (Romans 8:19 NKJV).

Where God's presence is, His blessings are also, along with the miracles of God. We can go to that holy place through our praise, a place where there is no longer a veil separating us from entering into the power, the blessings, and the anointing. When Jesus was crucified, the veil of the temple was rent in twain. It was torn in half from the top, indicating that it was God who did the tearing.

David said in Psalm 100:4: "Enter into his gates with thanksgiving, and into his courts with praise: be thankful unto him, and bless his name."

Praise brings God's presence, victory, healing, deliverance and the peace of God that surpasses all understanding. So we need to sacrifice not a lamb, nor the blood of goats or the ashes of a heifer because, once and for all, Jesus was the supreme sacrifice for sins. We, as priests unto the Lord, ought to give spiritual sacrifices.

We are a royal priesthood, a chosen generation of a strange and peculiar people! The Bible says in 1 Peter 2:5, "you also, as living stones, are being built up a spiritual house, a holy priesthood, to offer up spiritual sacrifices acceptable to God through Jesus Christ" (NKJV).

Still, men and women can walk in the anointing. We see it in the lives of others, such as William Branham, Jack Cole, A.A. Allen, Aimee McPherson, Benny Hinn, and many others.

I recall hearing about a man who was in a church service, and the pastor prayed for a baby he was holding. That man was lost. He said the anointing went through the baby and into his body, changing his life. It can do the same for you and change your life forever!

The anointing is tangible, and it is transferable. You can feel it, and you can taste it. That is why the Bible says in Hebrews 6:4-6 (NKJV): "For it is impossible for those who were once enlightened, and have tasted the heavenly gift, and have become partakers of the Holy Spirit, and have tasted the good word of God and the powers of the age to come, if they fall away, to renew them again to repentance, since they crucify again for themselves the Son of God, and put Him to an open shame."

We read also in Hebrews 2:1-4: "Therefore we ought to

give the more earnest heed to the things which we have heard, lest at any time we should let them slip. For if the word spoken by angels was stedfast, and every transgression and disobedience received a just recompence of reward; how shall we escape, if we neglect so great salvation; which at the first began to be spoken by the Lord, and was confirmed unto us by them that heard him; God also bearing them witness, both with signs and wonders, and with divers miracles, and gifts of the Holy Ghost, according to his own will?"

We find in 2 Kings 13:20-21 that a man of God, Elisha, was dead and had been dead so long that there was no flesh remaining upon the corpse. Only the bones remained. There was a band of Moabites in the land who had a dead man on their hands. Unknowingly, they threw the body into Elisha's sepulcher, or grave, and when it touched Elisha's bones, the man arose back to life!

The anointing can become so strong in you that it penetrates your muscles and even your bones. Without the anointing, you will never be effective. Even though God had chosen David to be king, he sent Samuel to anoint him because he needed the anointment to be effective.

Just as he was physically anointed with oil, we are all spiritually anointed with the Word of God. Sometimes we are physically anointed, being symbolic of the Spirit.

My heart's desire is that after reading this book, you will

desire to have a much closer walk with Jesus, who was the Word made manifest in the flesh.

Oral Roberts once stated, "I believe that Christianity isn't a formal stylized religion but a whole way of life that touches everything we do. The Christian expects God to use him as an instrument, healing the hurts and pains of others."

You see the anointing isn't just for you. It is to help God's people destroy the hurts and pains of everyday life. That is why the book of Isaiah says in 61:1: "The spirit of the Lord God is upon me; because the Lord hath anointed me ..." This is the same Scripture that Jesus preached in the temple, letting us know that we will never be very effective without the anointing. If God calls you to the ministry, He will anoint you because you will never be effective to those whom God has sent you to minister to without it.

There are deeper depths and higher heights in God! The prophet Ezekiel saw in a vision the wheel in the middle of a wheel. There is a church within the Church. There are they who are satisfied in God just where they are, but there are others who want a closer walk with God.

Many of God's people have waded out into the anointing ankle deep, some knee deep, and some waist deep. But this book is intended for those who want to walk out until the waters of God's anointing cover their lives.

This is found in Ezekiel 47:4-5: "Again he measured a thousand, and brought me through the waters; the waters were to the knees. Again he measured a thousand, and brought me through; the waters were to the loins. Afterward he measured a thousand; and it was a river that I could not pass over: for the waters were risen, waters to swim in, a river that could not be passed over."

Remember also what the Bible says in Ezekiel 31:4: "The waters made him great, the deep set him up on high with her rivers running round about his plants, and sent her little rivers unto all the trees of the field." The deep set him up on high. Psalm 42:7 (NKJV) tells us: "Deep calls unto deep at the noise of Your waterfalls; all Your waves and billows have gone over me." You have to get into deep places with God to reach those who are deep in sin.

This anointing will splash out onto the lives of others when you get full. Most anointed ministers come out from under other anointed ministers, even if there is a call of God on their life.

God called Moses but sent him to the house of Jethro, his spiritual leader, or pastor. Jethro taught Moses about the God of Abraham, Isaac, and Jacob.

Look at the ministry of the Apostles and how great and anointed they were. They came out of Jesus' ministry, who was the Word manifested in the flesh. If you are not faithful to a church, you will never pastor one. God is looking for faithful people to serve Him.

The things I have written in this book are to help you

obtain and walk in the anointing. Remember, God cannot bless what is cursed.

Malachi 3:9 tells us: "Ye are cursed with a curse: for ye have robbed me, even this whole nation." God cannot bless what is cursed. Neither can any man curse what God has blessed!

Anointed children of God pay their tithes!

Chapter Three

If we walk in the anointing, we will not fulfill the lusts of the flesh. We can choose to do nothing, but if we choose to sit in the seat of do-nothing, we will never walk in the anointing.

When we sit in good church services under very anointed preaching, faith comes alive in our hearts because faith comes by hearing first and hearing by the Word of God. We say within ourselves that when I get out of this service, I am going to do more for God. I am going to fast, pray more, study, and seek God's face. But as soon as we leave, we forget and don't do anything, or we do very little of these things.

Jesus spoke a parable about a sower who sowed seeds. Some fell on good ground. Good ground is the one who, having heard the word, does it. They are the ones who walk in the anointing. He said some fell among the thorns, and some just fell on the ground. These are the ones who hear the word and believe but fail to act upon it. These will not walk in the anointing of God. That is why Jesus said some bear thirty-fold, some sixty-fold, and others one hundred-fold fruit. I pray that you are not a hearer only but a doer of the word! Doers obtain the anointing.

We are spiritual beings. As a child of God, you are not your own. God can and will use you knowingly as well as unknowingly. Peter walked down the street unknowingly and then realized that God was using his shadow to heal the people around him.

I heard a story some time ago about a man of God who was in a revival service. The service was over, and people were leaving and shaking hands. This particular night of the revival, there was a young boy who had badly crossed eyes. The young boy had his back to the man of God. Unknowingly, the man patted some of the kids on the head. When he touched this boy, his eyes were made straight! As the young boy turned and looked at the man of God, he asked, "What can I do for you, young man?" The people standing there told him that when he touched the boy's head, his eyes went perfectly straight.

I pray God will open your understanding to the anointing. If you attend a church, and people leave like they came in, that is not a true church. When people come bound and leave just as they came, it is only a social gathering. Church is a place where God meets the needs of His people! It is a place where the discouraged leave encouraged, where the bound leave free, and where the lost leave saved and forgiven of their sins. If you are not seeing this in the church you are attending, the glory of the Lord has departed. Get out of that place, and get to some place where God is moving, where He is being praised and lifted up, a place where you can grow in God and in His anointing.

The Scriptures say that God confirms His Word with signs following. When a man of God preaches the Word of God, God will confirm it by someone being saved, set free, or healed by the divine healing power of God.

The Bible tells us in Mark 16:20: "And they went forth, and preached every where, the Lord working with them, and confirming the word with signs following. Amen."

Because the letter (the law) kills, God's Word came not just in word but in spirit and power.

God still saves, heals, and sets free. Beware of people or ministries who tell you God only moved in the past or who make excuses about why God is not moving today. If their god does not save, heal, or set free, they are serving a dead god. We serve a Living God who is true. Jesus is His name.

Watch out for people who make excuses. God is still in business and more than able to bless your life. Luke 12:32 says, "Fear not, little flock; for it is your Father's good pleasure to give you the kingdom." God wants you to walk in his blessings and anointing!

Acts 10:38 says, "How God anointed Jesus of Nazareth with the Holy Ghost and with power: who went about doing good, and healing all that were oppressed of the devil; for God was with him." You will never cast out devils without the baptism of the Holy Ghost and His anointing in your life. Not the Holy Ghost someone taught you to say, "Repeat after me." NO! I am talking about the Holy Ghost that came out of your belly like rivers of living waters, unknown tongues that just began to roll out of your mouth.

When the anointing is present in a service, you stand in a place of authority. Where the anointing is present, miracles are taking place. When the anointing is so real and present, do not leave until it lifts because, at that time, you are in a great place with God to receive your miracle!

Chapter Four

10 Steps to Obtaining the Anointing

1. You must be born again and baptized by water. What is born of the flesh is flesh, but what is born of the Spirit is spiritual.
2. You must be filled with the Holy Ghost. This is the evidence of speaking with unknown tongues.
3. You must have a very strong prayer life and study time.
4. Be faithful to a local assembly.
5. You must lay aside every weight and sin that may so easily beset you.
6. You must walk worthy of God. Jesus said in Matthew 10:37-39: "He who loves father or mother more than Me is not worthy of Me. And he who loves son or daughter more than Me is not worthy of Me. And he

who does not take his cross and follow after Me is not worthy of Me. He who finds his life will lose it, and he who loses his life for My sake will find it."

I met a man a while back who had made a profession of faith a long time before, but he would not give up the things in his life that were bad. It was not long before he backslid. God spoke to me and said, "He was not worthy of me!" I questioned God about it. God said, "He was not willing to forsake all and follow me!"

7. Be faithful even in hard and trying times because your problems or circumstances will not move God. God cares about them, but it is **your faith** that moves God!

8. If you want to obtain the anointing, care about the needs of God's people more than your own needs. You see, it's not all about you, but it's about helping others. If you care about them, God will take care of you.

9. Have no oughts in your heart against any man! Serve God out of a pure heart.

10. Last but not least, don't think less of yourself. Don't let the devil make you feel less than you really are. Ignore his lies that say you will never amount to anything, you never graduated, you were abused as a child, you have no education, or you have a learning disability.

   If the devil can make you feel less, you will never walk in the anointing. **I charge you, in the name of**

Jesus, to rise to your feet and shake your fists in the face of the devil. Make your face like flint, and be a champion for the Lord! This is what God intended for you to do.

Let us walk as obedient children of the light! We can learn from biblical characters. They are in the Bible for our examples. I am reminded of King David. His only job was shoveling sheep dung. He wasn't qualified to be king, but God chose him to be king. He was the apple of God's eye and very anointed because he sang praises unto God, not to be heard of man! Let's get alone with God each and every day and take time to praise Him. We need to have the right relationship with God.

Judas was one of the original twelve disciples who had a relationship with Jesus, but it was not the right one. Why, you ask? Because when he did wrong by betraying Christ, he did not repent from his heart. He was just sorry he got caught.

Peter was also one of the original twelve, and when he did wrong by denying Christ, he repented in his heart and was forgiven, unlike Judas who is in hell. God isn't looking for someone with great talent but someone to serve Him out of a pure heart!

Chapter Five

The anointing is not obtained overnight. It takes time. The Scriptures say that "one sows and one waters, but it is God who gives the increase" (1 Cor. 3:6). As we grow in our relationship with God, we grow in the anointing. God will never anoint that which He will not use. If God has anointed you, you can be sure He will use you.

There are many ways we can be used of God! We think if we are not in the pulpit, we are not being used of God. But where are the anointed prayer warriors, the choir leaders, etc.?

A big part of having the anointing is understanding the purpose of having it in your life. A lot of times we see people receive prayer, after which they are healed. Maybe they could not walk, and after prayer, they could. They say they know God healed them, for they were unable to walk before, but they are still in pain. If you are healed under the anointing, you can overcome your afflictions in the flesh. Proverbs 18:14 tells us, "The spirit of a man will sustain him in sickness, but who can bear a broken spirit?"

God has anointed people in all denominations, so if you think you are the only one that God has anointed, you are fooling yourself.

God is bigger than we can preach him! The cross is much bigger than that. The anointing will transform you into a supernatural, and greater, spiritual being.

Acts 2:17 says: "And it shall come to pass in the last days, saith God, I will pour out of my Spirit upon all flesh ..." We do not have to wait for God to send some prophet, even though God can and has done that. We just have to get in that place with God to receive the blessings He has to give.

There are different levels of the anointing. There's a thirty-fold anointing, a sixty-fold anointing, and a hundred-fold anointing. Let us walk worthy before God to obtain that one hundred-fold anointing. It is being poured out now, in these last days! But God cannot pour something holy into something unholy. As you cannot put new wine into old wineskins lest they burst during fermentation, God will not put His anointing in someone who is defiled by sin.

"Know ye not that ye are the temple of God, and that the Spirit of God dwelleth in you? If any man defile the

34

temple of God, him shall God destroy; for the temple of God is holy, which temple ye are" (1 Cor. 3:16-17). If any man defiles the temple, God will destroy him.

Which temple are you?

Let those of us who have the talent to play the guitar, piano, harmonica, etc., go somewhere today and take time just to play or sing Jesus a personal song. We, as servants of the Most High God, are His sons and daughters. As a young man, maybe you carried firewood for your dad. You would stack the wood as high as you could because you wanted him to be proud of you. Don't you think it would have meant more if you had carried in your usual amount and went to your dad and put your arms around him and said, "Dad, I love you!"

God is looking for His children to tell Him that they love Him every day! Yet, we get so busy, caught up in our ministries and everyday life that we forget to take time to worship God and tell Him that we love Him. If you're too busy for that, then you're too busy for Him to love you.

Chapter Six

God does not measure the stature of a man by his appearance, for the outward man perisheth. You may look and say, *Why would God use them*? Maybe they're tall, or maybe they're short. Remember that God does not see man as we see man. Man looks on the outward appearance, but God looks at the inside of a man.

People are so bad about judging others for things they have no control over, like the color of someone's skin. We cannot choose to be born of a certain race, nor can we choose to be born without defects. We should look at people as God would look on them.

The closer we get to God in our relationship with Him, the more we begin to see with the eyes of compassion as He does. We need to be looking beyond the flesh and seeing the hurts and pains of God's people. We need to see a lost and dying humanity that needs a Savior.

Oral Roberts once said, "Remember, the Bible teaches us that God is holy and can't tolerate sin. Sin separates us from God. Sin is the root of all trouble, illness, and problems. God will not anoint the soul that sinneth. The soul that sinneth shall surely die."

A good sign that you are on the right track to obtaining the anointing is that you will have a love/hate relationship involved in your life. You will love righteousness, and you will hate sin. Your devotion to God will know no bounds, and your love for Jesus cannot be described. Your only desire will be to please him!

I pray that this book challenges you to do more for God. I challenge you to purpose in your heart to do more. You cannot think your way to God, nor to heaven. Neither can you think your way to the anointing. Wisdom alone will not do it. You must use your heart. Christ shared in our humanity so that we might share in His divinity.

The Bible tells us in Hebrews 1:9: "Thou hast loved righteousness, and hated iniquity; therefore God, even thy God, hath anointed thee with the oil of gladness above thy fellows." Let us, as good stewards of God, not speak badly about God's anointed. "Who shall bring a charge against God's elect? It is God who justifies" (Romans 8:33 NKJV).

Three times in the Bible Jesus wept—at Lazarus' tomb, in the Garden of Gethsemane, and over Jerusalem. Why did he weep over Jerusalem? He said, "O Jerusalem, Jerusalem, the one who kills the prophets and stones those who are sent to her!" (Matt. 23:37a, Luke 13:34a NKJV).

It breaks God's heart when we criticize His man. When we talk badly about him, we spiritually stone him. These things ought not be done. When you get saved, the Anointer, Christ, comes to live inside of you, and He has a way of getting the anointing out of you. We keep looking for the anointing to come, but the anointing is already in you if you are born again. God uses situations to pull the anointing out of a person, so they can be a blessing to others.

When someone makes wine, they put pressure on the grapes to get the juice out. God uses the things that war against us to cause us to fight, to get the anointing out of us. It takes pressure to release what is inside of us, just like the grapes.

The Scriptures often refer to us as trees. You are either an olive tree or a corruptible tree. Revelation 11:3-4, states, "And I will give power unto my two witnesses, and they shall prophesy a thousand two hundred and threescore days, clothed in sackcloth. These are the two olive trees, and the two candlesticks standing before the God of the earth."

In Ecclesiastes 11:3 it says, "If the clouds be full of rain *[representing the anointing]*, they empty themselves upon the Earth *[God's creation-His people]*, and if the tree fall toward the south, or toward the north, in the place where the tree falleth, there it shall be." God has cast our sins as far as the east is from the west. Do not listen to the devil's lies and dabble in sin, for sin brings forth death. Spiritually speaking, don't fall toward the north or the south.

In Mark 8:24, the blind man said, "... I see men as trees, walking." We think maybe he could not see very well, but perhaps he could see all too well! So Jesus touched him again.

We need to be an olive tree full of God and his anointing, not a corruptible tree full of sin. If you live right and do what God commands of you, you will be meat for the Master's use, someone whom God can and will use.

After God destroyed the earth with water, Noah sent forth a raven, and he returned not, for it was a flesh-eating bird. Then he sent out a dove, and it returned having no place to perch. Then he sent out another a dove, and it returned, not with a dogwood or an oak branch, but with an olive branch.

When the dove returned with the olive branch in its beak, I believe God was showing Noah that he was still His anointed, and his blessings were before him.

I believe the reason you have obtained this book is because you desire to be an olive tree and to be God's anointed to walk in faith and in power!

A lot of things take place when you get saved. Sometimes you will face spiritual battles, but do not become discouraged.

It is God preparing you to be a walking, talking, breathing, living sanctuary. We need to be vessels that God can use to pour His anointing into until it is overflowing into someone else's life. You see, God's sanctuary is not a building or a tent; it is you, you are the temple of the living God!

You need to ask God today, *Lord, prepare me to be a sanctuary.* God wants you pure and holy, tried and true, just like the song says. Serve God in the beauty of holiness, remembering that angels bow before him. They rest not, day or night, praising Him always! Ask yourself today, *Am I a sanctuary? Would God want to live within me?*

Mark 11:25 states: "And whenever you stand praying, if you have anything against anyone, forgive him, that your Father in heaven may also forgive you your trespasses."

Do you have ought in your heart against another? Do you have strife, envy, anger, sin, or maybe even jealousy? If you have any of these things in your heart, I can say with boldness that you are not the type of sanctuary that God would want to dwell in! Repent now, and turn from those things, so God can forgive you of your trespasses and make you a clean vessel. We must approach the throne of God with boldness, and any kind of sin prevents that from happening. But repentance clears the pathway to God.

Let us walk and live in the anointing daily! "If we live in the Spirit, let is also walk in the Spirit" (Gal. 5:25). Verses 16-18 tell us: "Walk in the Spirit, and you shall not fulfill the lust of the flesh. For the flesh lusts against the Spirit, and the Spirit against the flesh; and these are contrary to one another, so that you do not do the things that you wish. But if you are led by the Spirit, you are not under the law."

We do not have to go around worried all the time about breaking one of the Ten Commandments of God because we are not led of the flesh as in times of old, but we are led by the Spirit. The Old Testament was only a shadow of better things to come.

People who lie, cuss, cheat, or steal are not led of the Spirit. "But the fruit of the Spirit is love, joy, peace, long-suffering, kindness, goodness, faithfulness, gentleness, self-control. Against such there is no law. And those who are Christ's have crucified the flesh with its passions and desires. If we live in the Spirit, let us also walk in the Spirit. Let us not become conceited, provoking one another, envying one another" (Gal. 5:22-26 NKJV).

Against such there is no law! Even though our bodies decay and die, we will live forever if we believe that Christ died for our sins. Sometimes you may feel that God is so far away, but He is not! God knows your thoughts and the very intents of your heart. The next time you feel like a failure, remember that He has engraved you in the palm of His hand. If we live right, serve God, and keep His commandments, we will abide in the shadow of the Almighty.

As I write this with pen in hand, God said tell them:

"Behold, the tabernacle of God is with men!"

Revelation 21:3 says, "And I heard a great voice out of heaven saying, Behold, the tabernacle of God is with men, and he will dwell with them, and they shall be his people, and God himself shall be with them, and be their God."

People love the anointing and seeing someone operating under the anointing. They want it, but they do not want to hear about due process.

We live in such a fast-paced society, fast food, fast cars, microwaves, etc., that we think God is like that. You will never get on the roof without first using a ladder. If you want a rooftop anointing, you will have to walk the way God has ordained in His Word. Walk the way Jesus walked!

John 8:31 (NKJV) says, "Then Jesus said to those Jews who believed Him, 'If you abide in My word, you are My disciples indeed.'"

Ask yourself, *Why do you want the anointing?* Some people pray, fast, and study for the anointing because they want it. It is not just for the Jews. It is for the purpose of helping God's people. We need to have the right motivation when seeking God for the anointing. God will share His glory with no one!

The Mount of Olives is set apart from Jerusalem. It is east of Jerusalem, about a Sabbath day's journey. If God has anointed you, it is because He has set you apart for His work. The Bible refers many times to the Mount of Olives.

Jesus taught on many occasions from the Mount of Olives. This place represents the anointing. It is set on a hill. You should be that city that is set on a hill. If you have Jesus Christ, the Giver of Life, the Anointer, living in you, then people can't help but notice Him in your life. Let the light of the glorious gospel shine in you. If He is in you, He will shine on the outside, too. Jesus on the inside will work on the outside. You can see miracles today just like those in times of old because God is not gone.

If we will humble ourselves and pray and seek His face diligently, then we will hear from heaven and see the miracles of God in the body of Christ (see 2 Chr. 7:14). The wheelchairs will be empty, the crutches broken. There will come a power of authority that will shake the foundations of the churches.

We are living in a better day of miracles than any time the church has ever seen. The Bible tells us that better is the ending than the beginning (Ecc. 7:8). Better is the end of all things than the beginning thereof.

Chapter Seven

We, as anointed sons and daughters, need to place a demand on the anointing. I see more often than not people placing a demand on the anointing and wondering why God does not move! That is because they are seeking the ministry but not seeking God first. They are working on their ministry but not working on their relationship with God. If you seek first the kingdom of God and His righteousness, all these things will be added unto you (see Matt. 6:33).

We live in a society today where people place themselves in ministry, but when God calls you and anoints and commissions you to speak for Him, there is an opening of your understanding. There is a revealing of His Word to you from that day when God calls you. You cannot speak His words until He first speaks it into you. He has to speak it to you before you can speak it to His people.

What we need to understand about the anointing is that men of God can only release or minister to you what is in their own spirit from God. This is why you may see those who pray for someone, and they are not touched. Then someone else prays for them, and their lives are changed forever. When someone whom God has not called ministers to you, you are not changed. But when God has anointed someone, and he prays for you or ministers to you, you have a different outlook on life.

The anointing that God wants to pour out into you, and into all of us, is not just to make us feel good. It is to change our outlook on life. God has anointed people who cause change by just being around them. Even though you may have left their presence, something got down inside of you and changed your outlook. That which once looked impossible now looks possible, and what looked like defeat now looks like victory because of the anointing in their life.

God lives in the tent of our bodies, in our spirits, so live honorably and walk uprightly before God, knowing that one day you will put off the tent of this body, and the spiritual man will live with Him forever throughout eternity. So let the rivers of living waters flow out of you.

If you give yourself to unrighteousness, you will be a well without water, a cloud that is carried about with the tempest. But if you walk righteously, the anointing will be in you as a well of living water to pour out over God's people, His heritage.

I call to your remembrance when God spoke to Samuel the prophet and said, …"How long will you mourn for Saul, seeing I have rejected him from reigning over Israel? Fill your horn with oil, and go; I am sending you to Jesse the Bethlehemite. For I have provided Myself a king among his sons."

I am reminded of a time when God Himself filled His horn with oil and arose and poured it out upon a hundred and twenty souls in the upper room on the day of Pentecost. That anointing still remains today. The Bible said that when Samuel anointed David, the Spirit came upon him that day, and there it remained, just like it came on the day of Pentecost, and it still remains upon God's people today.

This book is a word in season that God wants you to know. It is a message for this hour to His people. God wants to activate His anointing in you to pour out onto those around you. In the Spirit, you become God's hands and feet.

The Bible says God breathed life into man in the Garden of Eden, and man became a living soul. When you get saved, God breathes into you His Spirit of Life, just as He breathed life into Adam, and you become alive in the Spirit. God breathes the breath of life because He is the Giver of life. Without God's breath, or Spirit of Life, in you, you are dead.

We need to be driven and allow the Holy Spirit to drive

us into a great and lasting relationship with Christ today. If Christ was driven by the Holy Spirit, we also need to be driven by the Holy Spirit.

Conclusion

Maybe you have read this book and don't know Jesus Christ as your personal Savior and Lord, or you're not one hundred percent sure that if you died today you would be with him. Please pray right now!

Say, "Lord Jesus, I confess that I am a sinner in need of a Savior. I believe You died for me and arose from the dead on the third day by the power of God. Rise up in my heart and be my personal Savior and Lord. I'm through with the devil! I accept Jesus Christ into my heart and believe that I am saved!"

Now, tell the devil, "Devil, I am saved!"

If you prayed that prayer, you are in store for an awesome journey! Billy Graham once said that when you get saved, you actually become a new creature. There comes the implementation of the divine nature of God in you, and you become a partaker of God's own life. Jesus Christ, through His Spirit, takes up residence in you.

Final Thoughts

I believe that every time you read this book, you will learn and grow more in the anointing and in your relationship with God! You can choose not to do anything and lay this book aside, but if you do, then this book has been a waste of your time. Or, you can say it might work for some people, but it's not for you. If you do that, you will miss the anointing of God and the miracles He has for your life.

You can, however, take the teaching I have given in this book and walk in God's anointing. God will do what He says He will do. He will do it regardless of your choices. I can guarantee you by the authority of God's Word that if you will do as I have instructed in this book, you will grow stronger in the anointing every day!

May God bless you, in the name of the Lord and Savior, Jesus Christ.

Praise the Lord!

I hope that this book, *Obtaining The Anointing: It is for you!* is a blessing for you and your family. I pray that it will encourage you to want to do more for God and that it will cause you to want to grow in the anointing.

I believe that you have not obtained this book by chance, that it has been placed to propel you into a closer walk with God. That is why I have written this book, to encourage God's people to want a closer walk and a greater walk with Him. I stand on the belief that Jesus Christ was not only the Son of God, but He *was* God, according to 1 Timothy 3:16:

> **"And without controversy**
> **great is the mystery of godliness:**
> **God was manifest in the flesh,**
> **justified in the Spirit,**
> **seen of angels,**
> **preached unto the Gentiles,**
> **believed on in the world,**
> **received up into glory."**

Your Brother in Christ,
Keith Ingram

REV. KEITH INGRAM

REV. KEITH INGRAM is an ordained minister located in the Upper East Tennessee area. Having been raised by a devoted Christian mother, he has been in ministry for much of his adult life and has a burden to see the body of Christ matured and walking in power and authority under the anointing of the Holy Spirit. He has pastored several churches and is currently serving God in numerous evangelistic endeavors.

Keith and his wife, Rachel, have two grown children, Canaan and Nichole, and several grandchildren.

www.ingramcontent.com/pod-product-compliance
Lightning Source LLC
Chambersburg PA
CBHW061159040426
42445CB00013B/1738